Oliver Herford

An Alphabet of Celebrites

Oliver Herford

An Alphabet of Celebrites

1st Edition | ISBN: 978-3-75237-073-7

Place of Publication: Frankfurt am Main, Germany

Year of Publication: 2020

Outlook Verlag GmbH, Germany.

Reproduction of the original.

AN ALPHABET OF CELEBRITIES

CELEBRITIES

Oliver Herford

'S

Albert Edward, well meaning but flighty,

Who invited King Arthur, the blameless and mig

To meet Alcibiades and Aphrodite.

is for Bernhardt, who fails to awaken

Much feeling in Bismarck, Barabbas, and Baco

is Columbus, who tries to explain

How to balance an egg—to the utter disdain

Of Confucius, Carlyle, Cleopatra, and Cain.

C

D

'S

for Diogenes, Darwin, and Dante,

Who delight in the dance Of a Darling Bacchant

is for Edison, making believe

He's invented a clever contrivance for Eve,

Who complained that she never could laugh in h

F

is for Franklin, who fearfully shocks

The feelings of Fenelon, Faber, and Fox.

is Godiva, whose great bareback feat

Though Gounod and Goldsmith implore and ent

H

is for Handel, who pours out his soul

Through the bagpipes to Howells and Homer, w

On the floor in an ecstasy past all control.

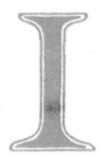

is for Ibsen, reciting a play

While Irving and Ingersoll hasten away.

is for Johnson, who only says "Pish!"

To Jonah, who tells him his tale of a fish.

K

is the Kaiser, who kindly repeats

Some original verses to Kipling and Keats.

is Lafontaine, who finds he's unable

To interest Luther and Liszt in his fable,

While Loie continues to dance on the table.

is Macduff, who's prevailed upon Milton

And Montaigne and Manon to each try a kilt on

is Napoleon, shrouded in gloom,

With Nero, Narcissus, and Nordau, to whom

He's explaining the manual of arms with a broom

is for Oliver, casting aspersion

On Omar, that awfully dissolute Persian,

Though secretly longing to join the diversion.

is for Peter, who hollers "No! No!"

Through the keyhole to Paine, Paderewski, and

is the Queen, so noble and free—

For further particulars look under V.

R

'S

Rubenstein, playing that old thing in F

To Rollo and Rembrandt, who wish they were d

'S

is for Swinburne, who, seeking the true,

    the good, and the beautiful, visits the Zoo

Where he chances on Sappho and Mr. Sardou,

And Socrates, all with the same end in view.

T

is for Talleyrand toasting Miss Truth,

By the side of her well, in a glass of vermouth,

And presenting Mark Twain as the friend of his

is for Undine, pursuing Ulysses

And Umberto, who flee her damp, death-dealing

is Victoria, noble and true—

For further particulars look under Q.

'S

Wagner, who sang and played lots for

Washington, Wesley, and good Doctor W

His prurient plots pained Wesley and Watts,

But Washington said he "enjoyed them in spots.

is Xantippe, who's having her say,

His prurient plots pained Wesley and Watts,

And frightening the army of Xerxes away.

Y

is for Young, the great Mormon saint,

Who thinks little Yum Yum and Yvette so quai

He has to be instantly held in restraint.

is for Zola, presenting *La Terre*

To Zenobia the brave and Zuleika the fair,

Whose blushes they artfully conceal with their h

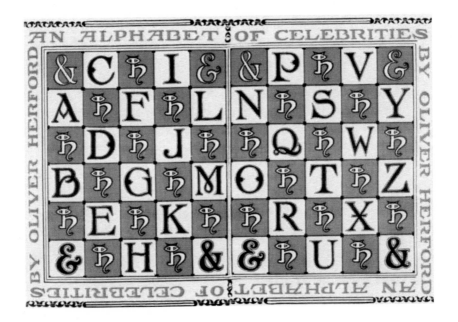